ROOSTER

in the

HEN HOUSE

Stories and Poems

Edited by:

John Newlin and Billie Travalini

ISBN: 9798615066344

Cover design by Karen Hurley-Heyman and Lois Hoffman

www.happyselfpublisher.com

Table of Contents

Introduction

"I write to discover what I know." Flannery O'Connor was convinced that writing requires us to value questions more than answers and to recognize that the journey is the meat of a story, not the destination. Writing also requires us to lop off a paragraph, or even a page, if the information is not moving the story forward. On many levels this makes writing much like math: the sum of the parts must equal the whole. There is no room for ego, or "extras" in the form of elevated language or wordiness.

We trust that the 10 stories and 19 poems in this anthology offer a new way of thinking about the process of writing and why daring to experiment—in voice and form—can make all the difference. While some of the stories and poems are not set in Delaware, all the participants are proud to call Delaware their home. It is Delaware's rich diversity and a willingness to see art as having a practical, as well as aesthetic value that sets Delaware apart. Stretching ninety-six miles along the eastern coast of the United States, Delaware was the first state to ratify the Constitution and one of four Border States during the Civil War. In the north of the state, the Quakers ran the Underground Railroad. In the south of the state, slave labor was common.

For a writer, the ability to see—through wide-open eyes-- why one person does one thing and another the opposite is essential. In Susan Towers' story, *Black Market Baby*, a daughter struggles to uncover the truth about her birth. Russ Reece's poem, "Last Dance: Elegy for a Great Blue Heron," relies on nature to teach us about ourselves and our surroundings as we come to recognize in the heron's final dance something at once familiar, and powerful. Sarah Burnett's story, **Summer, 1957,** uses Dodger baseball to set the scene for a time when fitting into Coney Island and Wall Street was not easy if you were young and female. In her flash fiction piece, *Caged*, Maria Masington delves into generational differences in a family where love is abundant and communication is reduced to scolding a Troll doll in a cage. In "San Francisco 1978-81," poet Irene Fick uses exacting detail and interesting phrasing to capture a time and place that is as visual as it is emotionally relevant, even today.

And, oh yes, this anthology is edited by a native Delawarean and a sometime New Englander. Billie Travalini was born and raised in Delaware, and John Newlin was born in Pennsylvania and lived many years in Massachusetts. This difference is in line with what it means to be Delawarean, where after World War II thousands of Southerners came to find jobs with Chrysler and General Motors, and others came from all over to work for DuPont and Hercules. All were seeking opportunities for upward mobility in a state where politicians answer their calls and friendship often begins with a nod of the head and "Good morning."

Of course this collection of writing is not intended to define Delaware, rather offer a window through which to see Delaware's emerging and professional writers doing what writers love to do: tell stories that stimulate thought, and, in doing so, help readers change the way they think in big ways and small.

John Newlin and Billie Travalini, co-editors

With Thanks

We're pleased to present *The Rooster in the Hen House*, the 2019 Delaware Division of the Arts anthology of stories, poems, and memoirs created by Delaware writers and poets who attended the Fall 2018 Seashore Writers' Retreat.

Preparing such an anthology is a complex undertaking, and we're thankful for the support of the Delaware Division of the Arts, and in particular, Roxanne Stanulis, who coordinated all the many details of hosting the retreat. We're also thankful to our mentors--- fiction writer, Leslie Pietrzyk, and poet Sandra Beasley, who led us through three days of stimulating workshops and craft lectures, and graciously allowed us to include their work in the anthology.

We're equally thankful to Karen Heyman-Hurley for her delightful cover design and to Milburn Orchard for allowing their handsome roosters to serve as our models.

We're enormously thankful to editor and publisher, Lois Hoffman, of The Happy Self-Publisher, who generously donated her expertise and many hours of hard work to the process of designing and printing this anthology. Without her, this anthology would not be possible.

Most of all we thank the writers and poets who bore with us through any number of edits and revisions and never ceased to remind us how artistically alive our state is, and how many talented literary artisans there are from the tip of New Castle County in the north to the Delmar border in the south.

One of the goals of this undertaking is to help make literary voices heard throughout Delaware. Many of the contributors to *The Rooster in the Hen House* will be reading from their work up and down the state in months to come. We hope you will take the opportunity to attend one or more of these readings. And now, enjoy the work of our fellow Delawareans.

John Newlin and Billie Travalini, co-editors

Credits

Some of the novel excerpts, short stories, and poems in this anthology have appeared in other publications and appear here by the permission of the author.

Barnett, Sarah. *Summer, 1957* is published here for the first time by permission of the author.

Beasley, Sandra. "The Translator" was first published in her collection, *I Was the Jukebox*, (W. W. Norton, 2010), and is reprinted here by permission of the author.

Chappelle, Sherry. "Milltown" was first published in *The Broadkill Review*, October, 2017, and is reprinted here by permission of the author. "Take Me Home" is published here for the first time by permission of the author.

Czerwinski, Melanie. *Memory* is published here for the first time by permission of the author.

Durborow, Christina. *Nunzi's Peccadilloes* is published here for the first time by permission of the author.

Fick, Irene. "Unfinished Things," was first published in *The Broadkill Review* July-August, 2018. "San Francisco 1978-81" was published in a slightly different form in *Philadelphia Stories*, 2013, and in her chapbook, *The Stories We Tell*, 2014. Both poems are reprinted here by permission of the author.

John, Gemelle. "If you count" was first published in a slightly different form in *Beltway Quarterly*, Fall, 2018. "If grief plural," was first published in *Beltway Quarterly, Fall, 2018.* Both poems are reprinted here by permission of the author.

Heyman, Karen H. "A Contraption Made of Dreams" and "You" are published here for the first time by permission of the author.

Kelts, Larry. "Rumbles & Reason Out of the North" and "Twisted Hair" are published here for the first time by permission of the author.

Lewes, TJ. *Rooster in the Hen House* is published here for the first time by permission of the author.

Masington, Maria. *Caged* is published here for the first time by permission of the author.

Morrell, Jennifer. *The Sky Flipped Upside Down* is published here for the first time by permission of the author.

Morris, Alice. "Because the Fox Crouches in the Street" and "I Tried So Hard Not To Write This Donut Poem" are published here for the first time by permission of the author.

Newlin, John. *Clean Up* is published here for the first time by permission of the author.

Pietrzyk, Leslie. *Something You're Proud Of* was first published in *Fork Lift, Ohio,* Issue #35-#36, Fall 2017, 99-103, and is reprinted here by permission of the author.

Reece, Russell. "Mambo," was published in a slightly different form in *The Avocet*, Winter, 2015, and is reprinted here by permission of the author. "The Last Dance: Elegy for a Great Blue Heron" is published here for the first time by permission of the author.

Sysko, LJ. "Battledore" was published in *Battledore, Finishing Line Press*, and in *New Women's Voices* series, 2017. "16" was published in *Battledore*; a previous version was published in *New York Quarterly*, 2011. Both poems are reprinted here by permission of the publisher.

Towers, Susan. *Black Market Baby* is published here for the first time by permission of the author.

Travalini, Billie. *On Hearing My Son Was Socrates and My Husband Frank Sinatra* was first published in *The Moth*, Spring, 2014, and is reprinted here by permission of the author.

Youkers, Jean. "Elegy for My Dad" and "Grandma's Apprentice" are published here for the first time by permission of the author.

This collection is dedicated to the writers of Delaware. It says a lot about the power of writing retreats: the power that comes from getting away from the ordinariness of everyday life and being with others who care as much about writing as you do. If also says a lot about having workshop leaders who lead with experience and patience and writers who see each other as being on the same journey and welcome the company, and the feedback. As with any successful retreat questions occur—lots of them—and answers follow: a powerful reminder that a retreat should be less about perfection and more about having the time and space to write uninterrupted and the willingness to embrace experimentation and feedback as valued steps in the process of *becoming better writers.*

The Smyrna Public Library is a member of the Delaware Division of Libraries. Founded in 1858, it moved into the Smyrna Opera House in 1870. Despite a destructive fire on Christmas night, 1948, the library thrives today.

Rooster in the Hen House

Walter Dunne perched precariously on a step stool as he rearranged the display, shifting the silk, cashmere, and angora to the top shelf. The shelves below sprouted an array of wool, cotton, and synthetic fibers, along with novelties like hemp and bamboo. He had been toiling on the restock since the shop had closed an hour earlier, and sweat sheened his forehead. Still, he smiled in anticipation of the following day while he focused on the new knitting needles in his cart.

Once at home, Walter fastidiously printed on a small slip of paper. He had spent a month considering the words, and his hands shook. He slipped the message into the pocket of his finest suit-coat, and then went to bed, exhausted but exhilarated.

Sunday morning whispered its way into Walter's dreams. Hopeful that the day's reality would be even better than his somnolence, Walter quickly got ready for work, double checking the note in his pocket before setting off. He opened the store a little early, even though he knew the woman of his dreams would not arrive until the afternoon. His heart raced just thinking about her weekly visit.

It was nearly one when the silver Buick pulled into the parking lot, and a tall lady in a fitted wool coat and silk scarf, wearing sensible heels, marched towards the store. Walter straightened his tie and opened the front door for his customer as always. He greeted her warmly as she entered, a hint of his Scottish brogue still evident despite his attempts at proper speech.

"Good afternoon, Lass. Welcome to ye."

"Good afternoon, Mr. Dunne. Has the new cashmere yarn arrived?"

"Aye, it has, as promised."

She smiled brightly and rushed down the central aisle towards the knitting section. Walter watched her a moment, appreciating how the light glinted off her hair and how her coat accentuated her waist. Then, he straightened his back and clasped his hands, waiting. Within seconds, he heard her gasp. Moments later, her sweet voice echoed off the walls.

"Mr. Dunne! Your assistance is needed in the knitting section, please."

He laughed himself down the aisle, admiring his customer. Her cheeks were flushed, adding a lovely glow to her pale skin. He controlled himself before speaking, his sparkling eyes alone betraying the serious demeanor of his countenance.

"Aye, Lass, what can I help ye with today?"

"The cashmere yarn, please. I'm afraid I can't reach it."

"Aye Lass, so sorry. We sell much more of the other fibers, ye see. Let me help ye get some down. Tis me pleasure to serve ye."

Walter grabbed the step stool, and quickly scaled it to grab skeins in the ten available colors. He held them as she inspected each one. He adored the way she grasped the yarn between her fingers, stroking gently one way, then the other, to get the feel of the fibers. She always closed her eyes when she did so, and he wondered what visions illuminated her darkness.

Her fingers accidentally brushed his arm when she caressed the last skein, an electric shock coursing between them.

She blushed, he laughed, and an awkward silence descended. At last, Evelyn spoke.

"I'll take four skeins of the camel color and two of the ivory, please."

"At once, Lass."

Walter ascended once more, returning the samples he shown her, and retrieving the desired yarn. He carried the items to the register and waited quietly, hands in pockets, while Evelyn perused the selection of knitting needles. As she bent to investigate the new bamboo needles, he slipped the piece of paper from his coat and slid it under the wrapping of the closest skein of yarn. His hands trembled and his heart pounded.

Evelyn approached the counter with the bamboo needles clutched in her hand, a look of surprise and delight on her face. She skipped the last step before laying her acquisition next to the register. Her voice was like caramel, syrupy and rich.

"Mr. Dunne, what lovely knitting needles you've stocked. The yarn will slide right off them!"

"Only the finest products for me finest customer."

Walter's voice shook slightly, and he busied himself with ringing up her order. He began to question the wisdom of his message. Never once had she flirted in any way, and never had he addressed her by name. Before he could recover the note, she shoved the last skein into the bag with the others and paid with exact change, her words a rush.

"Thank you so much, Mr. Dunne! I can't wait to get started. Have a lovely afternoon. Ta ta."

With that, she was out the door, leaving Walter alone with his worries.

Evelyn Frieden loved to knit, surrounded by her beloved chickens. As soon as she returned from shopping, she changed her clothes, turned on the radio, and took her seat by the fireplace. She grabbed the top skein from her bag of yarn, and began knitting at once, in tempo with Tchaikovsky. Knit stitch, knit stitch, purl stitch, knit. Yarn over, dip stitch, slip, slip.

She had completed four rows when the yarn stuck inside the skein. She tugged a few times, and then unwrapped the yarn to investigate. A folded piece of paper fluttered to the floor, black lettering peeking from inside. She stared at it, confused. At last, she seized the paper and read the message.

The moon glows pale next to my lassie's hair,
Its white and silver strands alight the gray,
Its texture fine like gossamer in air,
Like sunlight peeping on a cloudy day.

My lassie's skin is much like porcelain,
Exquisitely crafted throughout the years,
It's cracked and worn, a remnant of what's been,
With chips and spots, from smiling through the tears.

My lassie's body stands so straight and tall,
A fortress built to weather every storm,
So carefully she's constructed her wall,
But underneath cold stone, her heart beats warm.

And so, with hope, I knock upon her door,
A beggar with a dream and nothing more.

Please, join me for dinner?

Evelyn nearly dropped the paper. In all her years, she never had been so surprised. At first, she thought the message must be intended for someone else. Little by little, as she reread the lines, she saw herself in their description … gray hair, cracked skin, and a wall of stone.

Her next thought was to wonder about the author. She skimmed the letter again, and her eyes settled upon the word Lassie. She stared at the hens at her feet, and suddenly she knew.

"Clucky, I know who it's from! Mr. Dunne from the Craft Store has written a sonnet to me. Glory be, Chickira, I'm eighty-seven, far too old to court. Beyond that, Henrietta, he's at least ten years my junior. What would people say?"

None of the chickens responded, so Evelyn went into the kitchen to cook supper. She thought all during dinner, and throughout the night. The following morning, Evelyn went to the library to do some research. That night she talked to her chickens again.

"I always loved hugging my dear Erich, tucking my head up under his chin. I'd have to kneel to hug Mr. Dunne like that. Absurd isn't it, Hensel? I've established my way of life, and we're happy, don't you think, Chickenetta? It's better to just continue alone, right Popeye? O, Nugget, what would I ever do if I tried and it didn't work out?"

Nugget attempted to fly onto her lap, but flopped back to the floor. She picked up the bird and stroked her head.

"I guess if I try and fail, I'll just end up back in the same situation I have now. Perhaps that's not so bad. Thank you, ladies. I love you all. Now, the real question: Can Mr. Dunne love us all?"

Evelyn visited the Craft Store on Tuesday, Mr. Dunne's day off. She purchased several more skeins of yarn in purple, black, white, and sky blue, while chatting with the sales clerk, a twenty-something with thick glasses and thin lips.

"So, Allison, how do you like working here?"

"It's pretty great. Mr. Dunne always schedules around my college courses, and I even get a discount on supplies!"

"How lovely, dear. I imagine it can't pay very well though."

"Well, not a fortune, but it's above minimum wage, and I get unlimited vacation time. Mr. Dunne lets me take off whenever I need to travel home for the holidays, working the hours himself until I return. He's even letting me open Friday morning, so I can have off that night!"

Evelyn nodded thoughtfully, before bidding her goodbye. As she drove home, she thought about Mr. Dunne. Allison's description of his kindness was touching. A small smile played on Evelyn's lips while she considered the new bamboo knitting needles. She hadn't even asked for them, and yet he had anticipated her delight.

At home, Evelyn reread the sonnet, and then she opened her bag of new yarn. She knitted as quickly over the next two days, finishing late Thursday night. Friday morning, Evelyn strode into the Craft Store, a carefully wrapped package in hand, and collar pulled high against the bitter, January wind. A giggling Allison secreted the package into Mr. Dunne's office.

Several clients were in line when Walter arrived at the Craft Store shortly before 3:00 in the afternoon. He stashed his jacket under the counter and got to work, never entering his office until closing time. As he tallied the sales, his eyes fell upon a gift stashed underneath his desk.

He ripped open the paper breathlessly. Inside, he found a scarf, knitted with the Dunne Clan design in the colors of his family tartan. Along the bottom edge, the word YES was stitched in gold thread. Grinning wide, he wrapped the soft scarf around his neck, exposing a note written on the bottom of the box.

Join my girls and me for dinner at our house.
Saturday at 6:00. Address on the other side.

Walter arrived promptly the next evening, dressed in his finest suit and sporting his new scarf. He was nervous about his dinner date, and terrified about meeting her daughters. He knocked timidly upon the door. Inside, he thought he heard scratching and a distant clucking noise. Then, Evelyn opened the door.

"Good evening, Mr. Dunne. Welcome."

"Please, call me Walter."

"I'm glad you made it, Walter. Please, come in and meet my girls. Move over, General Tso."

With her foot, Evelyn nudged a chicken in a camouflage sweater out of the doorway. Walter could see at least ten more hens dressed in elaborate knitted clothes waiting inside the parlor. He paused a moment on the threshold.

"Walter, are you coming?"

"Aye Lass, why not. Only a fool would relinquish his opportunity to be the rooster in the hen house. Introduce me to yer bonnie bairns."

One by one, Evelyn presented each chicken to Mr. Dunne. He chuckled at their names, complimented their finely crafted clothing, and smiled broadly when Chickira danced right up to him. He didn't even mind when several hens lay on his feet during dinner.

Evelyn and Walter laughed for hours over their food. Neither could remember a livelier conversation. When it was time to go, Evelyn walked Walter to the door, and whispered hesitantly.

"So, you don't think I'm crazy?"

"Lass, yer aff yer heid, which is what I like best about ye. Be happy while yer living, yer a long time deid, after all."

Walter hugged Evelyn around the waist, pulling her tightly to him. She rested her chin upon his head, surprised by how comfortably it fit.

IRENE FICK

Unfinished Things

<u>Between 1963 and 1966</u>

The air — swollen with the promise of sex. We made out in a phone booth as he called home for a ride. Groped in the last row at the Holiday matinee. Did more in the sweaty back seat of his father's Ford. Or was it a Chevy? Thick soft lips (or were they thin and hard?) all over mine. He was tall. Short. His hair: dark, curly. No, blond, straight. There was a rumble below my belly.

<u>Late October 1984</u>

He raked only half of the forested front lawn before he went inside to watch football. A deep pile of leaves remained. Soon, family and friends would show up for the baby's christening.

<u>April 17, 1978</u>

I folded my maternity clothes, stored them in the guest room closet. Later, I watched new mothers at the mall hold babies against their breasts like merit badges.

<u>May 3 and 4, 1998</u>

Dad talked about his nausea from chemo and the new meds, but I half listened, pre-occupied. With what? The next call was from his wife, urging me to hurry.

<u>June 2016</u>

Each day, I cycled past the backyard of the big house with the in-ground pool. Each day, I saw the cage half-draped with canvas, heard the dog. I called Animal Control. They told me the old lab had water, food and shelter. Nothing they can do.

<u>Today</u>

The verse begins to drain itself of words, search for the right ending. The window inches closer to the sill. Soon, all the air will be on the other side.

IRENE FICK

San Francisco 1978-81

Adrift in my twenties, I dropped anchor
at a jelly bean house perched high on a slope,
stroked by fog, straddling salty bay bridges.
Stripped to my senses, I strolled into North Beach
cafés to hear Puccini crooned by paunchy old men
in spaghetti-stained aprons, sipped Pinot
on bare-bodied beaches, spent soulful afternoons
caressing Irish coffee at the Buena Vista,
flushed nights at fern bars downing drinks
under fuzzy lights. I pedaled my Schwinn
through the Presidio, sucked in the sea mist,
gazed into open-air joints jammed with wiry, wired
men. I clung to the margins of cable cars,
leaned into the sultry curves of fabled streets.
The City was on edge, caught between disco
and the hush of a deadly new virus. Yet,
I lingered, hoping to land on solid ground.

SUSAN TOWERS

Black Market Baby

Each time I look at the photograph, I remember my mother telling me children don't need their fathers after the age of seven.

She had a way of saying things that made me believe her. As a child, I believed her completely.

The photograph of me at seven is poster-size and set in an ornate baroque frame. Through the 1950s and 1960s, it hung in my mother's office in our family furniture store in Bakersfield, California. It was the first thing you saw when you walked in, hanging behind her big mahogany desk to let anyone sitting in one of the two chairs facing the desk know I was her daughter, just like the store was her store.

In the photograph, I am at a table in a nightclub in Havana, Cuba. My hair is pulled back in a ponytail and my smile is so broad you can see that my front teeth are too big for my face. I am wearing a fur-trimmed, white sweater over a gold satin dress. My hands are folded lady-like in my lap, and a gold bracelet is on my right wrist and a gold locket on a chain around my neck.

My mother took me to Cuba in 1957. I didn't realize until much later the significance of that trip. For me, it was exciting to be on an airplane and fly through clouds to a place I had never been. My memory holds patchy images of tropical foliage, banana trees and beaches, and pink Spanish-style buildings with wrought-iron balconies lining narrow city streets.

I see my mother in the back seat of a chauffeur-driven Cadillac convertible. She could be Loretta Young, with her dark curly hair and sheer scarf wrapped around her head and neck, and dark sunglasses hiding her deep brown eyes. I feel a warm breeze blowing against my face.

I sit in a nightclub, tasting the sugary sweetness of a Shirley Temple. I hear voices and see the lights turning onto the stage as a woman walks out to sing. I don't see who is sitting at the table with me.

In the daytime, the sun beats down. I pretend I am a horse galloping through the Nacional Hotel's manicured gardens and swimming in its huge pool.

One unsettling memory holds firm. I am in an open field and a soldier is picking up a kitten and squeezing it until blood runs out of its eyes and nose. I hear the soldier laugh and chase after me as I run away.

Our house is strangely quiet as my mother and I turn into the driveway. My father does not open the door. I sense his absence, but do not ask my mother why he isn't home. Velma, our maid, emerges and gives me a hug. I sink into her soft arms. I love her round face, kind smile, and gentle voice. She wears a floral dress and a plain apron that sways side-to-side as she walks back into the house.

After our return from Cuba, I remember the rush of water as Velma prepares my bath in the large bathroom at the end of the hall. There are bubbles, lots of bubbles.

My mother calls me into the bedroom she shares with my father. She hates the summer heat. We don't have central air-conditioning, and the shutters are drawn. The wallpaper is a swirl of black and rose. I sit on the quilted bedspread. I finger the soft swells of material held in place by tight stitching.

My mother's lips are crimson and she wears a string of pearls around her neck. Her short, black, curly hair stays in place. She wears a light-colored summer suit.

"Daddy doesn't live with us anymore. We're getting a divorce."

I can still hear the words. The shock brands me. A sharp pain gripping my abdomen.

"Children don't need their fathers after the age of seven," she says. "We'll be fine without him."

I look toward the bedroom door, willing it open to see my father emerge. I had never heard my parents argue. How could anything bad be happening? My mother, who runs the family furniture store, who is always busy, who never has time for me, is next to me. My father, who hugs me, plays with me, and lets me stand on his feet when he walks, is gone.

I scan the room. There is no sign of my father. No piece of clothing. No shoes. No glass of water or folded magazine on his bedside table. The closet door is ajar; his side is bare. The stabbing pain in my stomach intensifies.

My mother doesn't let up. She tells me about the origin of my birth. She says she wanted a baby but "your father couldn't have one."

"It was hard to find a healthy white baby after World War II," she added. "I had to hire a lawyer and it cost a lot of money."

"The lawyer found you," she says. "A black market baby because the lawyer didn't go through legal channels."

I'm not sure if she told me everything that day or if she disclosed details in later conversations, a little at a time, like a television serial drama. I came to believe I was purchased in the black market because my father was impotent.

My mother's voice drones on. I look at the mirror above her dresser and I see her image so large next to mine. She has driven my father away, I am certain of it. I stick my tongue out at the mirror. She sees me, turns, and slaps my face.

"How dare you!" My face hurts. Tears stream down my face onto the bedspread.

The sting of that slap is branded into my memory. Humiliation settles inside me like sludge at the bottom of a barrel. My mother pulls away from me and begins to cry. In a high-pitched voice, she says, "How could you? Don't you know I love you? Get out of here."

My ears are ringing. I run out of the bedroom. I can't run to my father. I can't run to Velma. My stomach hurts. I hold onto the pain. I do not want to be different from Joanne who lives down the street. I do not want to be a black market baby. I do not want to be another of my mother's purchases, like gold or fur. I want to run.

SANDRA BEASLEY

The Translator

He paid me to carry his words
in my mouth —
to give him the cut of sky,
the color of beef.
To give him please.
To give him thank you.
To give him tea kettle, spider, tango.
I ate at his table.
I moved into his basement.
I made a dictionary of sighs —
when to order takeout,
when to play Stravinsky, when
to tell the woman to take her clothes
and go. Soon he was dying.
I can't breathe, he said, so I said
I can't breathe. My heart, he said,
so I said My heart. It was my wrist
the nurse held, my chest
under the stethoscope. I'm sorry,
said the doctor, and my throat
became a coffin
they could not open.

Caged

My great-grandmother, Angela Pisano, a widow for sixty of her ninety plus years, lived alone in her condo among her oil paintings of Venice and family photos in gold leaf frames. In her powder room, embroidered hand towels read, **Preserve wild life, stay out all night,** even though I never saw her take a drink and she only stayed out all night when a family member was in the ER or in labor. In the middle of her dining room table, an 18-inch hookah, bought at a head shop in Wildwood because she thought it was a vase, held pussy willows and peacock feathers. Over her front door a Christmas card with the three kings promised protection from bad luck and fire. Of course, blessed palm fronds woven into crosses adorned every room.

When my great-grandmother reached 90, five of her seven children were still living, ranging in temperament and personality, some more of a pain in the neck than others. On one visit, I noticed something new on top of her refrigerator: a small decorative birdcage and inside was a vintage troll doll, who was naked and had neon blue hair.

Before I could ask, she pointed up, "Don't look at me Mike. You're bad, Mike — that's why you're in jail." I started laughing. Mike was a successful seventy-year-old business owner and family man who turned into a pouty seven-year-old when it came to his mother. After not speaking to her for a year, one day he magically appeared in the form of a troll incarcerated on top of her Frigidaire.

My great-grandmother didn't have Oprah or Dr. Phil. She didn't have twelve step programs or support groups. She didn't journal or air dirty linen in public. She had her parish priest, the angels, saints, her daughters, and a broken heart — so she coped the only way she knew how: she gave her troll son a piece of her mind whenever she needed to.

Thirty years later, I no longer have my great-grandmother, but I do have my own beloved, pain in the neck adult son. I have read books, talked to friends and worried about his feelings and self-esteem. I detached with love, loved unconditionally, embraced with radical acceptance, and worked on being an "actor," not a "reactor." But inside I longed to lash out, to tell him he was selfish and self-centered. I longed to tell him to pull his head out of his ass and grow up — but I knew it would be counter-productive.

When he forgot, or ignored, my fiftieth birthday, I coped the only way I knew how. I went on eBay and bought a small decorative birdcage and a vintage troll doll with neon lime green hair. He lives in the birdcage on top of my Kenmore fridge: His name is Tom.

KAREN HURLEY-HEYMAN

Contraption Made of Dreams

A Prose Poem

After plaid dresses, patent leather shoes, photos of sailors with tattoos; after ceramic panthers and parakeets that made life feel a little more exotic; after twirling hair in pin curls, learning how to throw a baton and catch it on the down spin; after reading comics while Dad read news; after hiding *The Grapes of Wrath* behind a hard-back *of Little Women*; after all that, I packed baloney sandwiches, chocolate chips, and Liberty dimes I'd saved to buy Tangee the invisible lipstick— and— I gave it all the slip.

What's left of that America pecks a kiss on my cheek when I return home to attend re-unions or funerals. Glancing into what once was a breakfast nook, I see a Better Homes and Gardens dining room, the small pane windows consumed by plate-glass sliding doors.

My last trip back, a wisp of Dad's ghost sat in his favorite chair. One knee crossed over the other, right elbow in the palm of his left hand, staring at wheels inside his skull still grinding out inventions: water wings stuffed into dynamite sticks that would explode to inflate if you needed to throw them at someone drowning in a swimming pool.

I saw myself, too, before school hunched in that chair pulled up to sunrise and an open oven door where I could warm my socks. *Shhhhh*, don't wake up the boys, Mom says, waiting for water to boil for our one cup each of Maxwell House Instant Brew.

Dad's chair made a sound of shattering glass, escaping canaries, a foot tangled in Schwinn spokes; the sound of peddling in the dark, high above sidewalks and rustling trees, a ghost-like fog circling street lamps; the grind of oiled gears. Balanced on last century's gigantic Penny farthing wheel, I didn't know how to stop, or climb down.

I've lived years now away from a square house on a slight hill in a small town. When I look across Willamette Valley at the opposing butte where the water tower still stands like a religious beacon shining down on people who had little to do with the world and nothing to do with the universe, I understand why Dad left his chair where he knew I'd sit in it; recall what seemed an inconsequential moment as a child, I climbed into his lap, looked out at the valley and realized I'd leave it someday on a contraption made of dreams.

KAREN HURLEY-HEYMAN

You

are not my only intimate.

Sometimes— I love
the little willow bent over the creek
just down the hill— as much as I love you.

SARAH BARNETT

Summer 1957

The summer of 1957 was the last summer of my childhood. The last summer the Dodgers played in Brooklyn. I did not go to Ebbets Field to see the Dodgers play one last time. I did not have a boyfriend. What I did have was a job and the beach.

At sixteen, I was two months away from college and working my first real job in the city, which to New Yorkers meant Manhattan. Each day I rode the subway from Brooklyn to a small office building off Fifth Avenue and took the elevator to the tenth floor where I had finagled my way into a secretarial spot at a wholesale clothing company.

After many unsuccessful attempts at finding summer employment, I became convinced that the only way to get a job was to tell three lies: (1) I was eighteen, (2) I wanted a permanent, full-time job, and (3) I could type sixty words per minute.

For the job interview, I wore the navy shirtwaist dress I'd worn to graduation. The office manager, was a timid man, whose white shirt struggled to button over his stomach, had about as much management experience as I had secretarial know-how. He accepted my story and hired me, omitting the usual typing test.

My friends, Marilyn and Sharon, had similar city jobs. For the first time in our lives we found ourselves in a world where no one was impressed by braininess. No one cared that we'd read Dostoevsky, solved simultaneous equations and conjugated French verbs. We put away book learning to type letters, file

41

reports, answer the telephone, and, hardest of all, without the wisecracking our classmates considered a mark of intelligence. Worse, we had to hide our abilities behind the secretarial persona we wore along with nylon stockings and dress shoes. I quickly learned there was no point correcting the grammar or writing style of any of my six bosses. If one of them wanted to describe a new dress line as "very unique" or confide to a client, "between you and I, Joe," I knew to leave it that way or suffer a lecture about wasting the firm's expensive coral-colored stationery on which erasures stood out like dandruff on a dark sweater.

Every Sunday, bathing suits under our clothes, the three of us took the subway across Brooklyn to the last stop at Coney Island. We'd cross the handball courts on Surf Avenue where shirtless men grunted and sweated as a small black ball hit the wall and rebounded with bullet-like force.

In high school, we spread our blankets at Bay 7, but we'd graduated to Bay 2, Brooklyn College territory. We were young for this crowd and knew we didn't belong. Thanks to a city-wide program, gifted students could skip a year of junior high, making Marilyn, Sharon, and me high school sophomores at thirteen, college freshmen at sixteen. Sure, we were smart, but our immaturity must have been as obvious as if we had worn our prom dresses to the beach—if we'd had prom dresses. We told ourselves that only kids not going to college would indulge in such frivolity. The truth was simpler: the boys we hung out with were every bit the misfits we were. And none of us could afford formal clothes, flowers, limos.

At Bay 2, we didn't want to stand out, but we didn't want to be invisible. Once we found a spot—stage right, not too far from the water—we spread out our blanket and anchored the corners with our shoes. Then we pulled out paperbacks or Modern Library editions of the classics. When the sun had warmed us almost to the point of discomfort, we headed for the water to swim, float and body surf.

Returning to the blanket to sunbathe, I could still feel the lift and pull of the waves. We'd eat the sun-warmed tuna salad sandwiches we'd packed, and then walk the shoreline, observing the touch football and volleyball games in the sand.

While I loved ocean swimming, I felt awkward in a bathing suit and wore one of my father's old dress shirts as a cover-up. Then there was my hair. Thick and curly, it refused to relax into the long, straight pony tail favored by popular girls. I settled for a "poodle cut," but considering the water, sun and humidity, I probably resembled a wire-haired terrier in need of a serious trim.

Back at Bay 7, the high school kids were listening to Elvis or to Pat Boone's "Love Letters in the Sand," but the college crowd had moved on to Pete Seeger or Miles Davis. If you were really with it, you brought a guitar or bongo drums and sat on the sand, improvising while others nodded appreciatively.

When I couldn't remember whether we tried to become part of a group, I emailed Sharon, who recalled bringing her ukulele and playing "Ain't She Sweet," the one song she knew. That only proved how naïve and unprepared we were for college life. "Wait till next year," we might have told ourselves, echoing the plaintive, and soon-to-be useless, sentiments of Brooklyn Dodgers fans.

Toward late afternoon, people began folding up blankets and hunting down stray shoes. We prolonged the day with dinner on the boardwalk, the menu always the same—a hot dog and a potato knish. Depression descended with the sun, as we anticipated Monday's subway ride and the workday monotony.

Since those long-ago days, the beach has been my refuge of choice. If I'm trapped somewhere— a dentist's chair, or enduring stop-and-go traffic—I try to recapture the buoyant feeling of floating atop ocean waves. Soon, I feel the sun on my shoulders and sand sifting through my fingers. Sometimes I even hear the bongos.

These days, I park my beach chair near the waves along the shoreline at Rehoboth Beach, Delaware. A floppy hat tames my hair. I no longer care how I look in a bathing suit.

I sit with a book and an iced tea watching the ever-changing, never-changing ocean. Rehoboth has become more than just my home; it is the place where I feel at home. A place to watch the sunset over Rehoboth Bay. A place where people greet me and Blue, my shelter mutt, as we walk the boardwalk. A place to meet and write with friends several times a week and read our work at large monthly gatherings.

One sunny day in July, as I relaxed in Cape Henlopen State Park, I saw them—three girls who looked like Marilyn, Sharon, and I once looked. One had curly hair—not stylish curly, but wiry, out-of-control brown ringlets springing from her head. Large sunglasses covered half her face. Another wore a voluminous cover-up and an unhappy expression that said this shirt isn't long enough to cover my thighs.

I watched the girls, hoping they'd race each other into the water, mentally urging my curly-haired counterpart to forget the mess the ocean would make of her hair and dive in. But all three stood at water's edge as if surprised to be at the beach.

Two weeks before Labor Day 1957, I entered my boss's cubicle and delivered my rehearsed speech, saying I'd just learned I'd received a scholarship and come September I'd be off to Brooklyn College. His calm response surprised me. I thought he might accuse me of taking the job under false pretenses. Instead, he congratulated me on my good fortune and wished me luck. Is it possible, I wonder now, that I'd spared him the hassle of firing an inept typist?

I headed for college, emerging four years later with a degree in mathematics and an unreliable boyfriend who worked as a musician. I was still on the shore, not quite ready to take the plunge into real life.

Years later, I would jokingly refer to July-August 1957 as "the worst summer of my life." Now, I see this as an exaggeration. Like the Dodgers' third place finish that year, the summer wasn't a total loss. The electric typewriter, Dictaphone and PBX switchboard are long obsolete, but I acquired other useful skills, such as detecting who was ready to pay the check and vacate a scarce lunch counter seat, and knowing where to position myself on the platform to grab an equally valuable subway seat. More importantly, I learned I'd rather dictate letters than type and file them.

Best of all, I learned that no matter how difficult life becomes, I can always escape to the beach. I do not need to hold a seashell to my ear to hear the ocean or the roar of roller coasters and the cries of riders. When I close my eyes, I see myself on a subway seat, a damp bathing suit under my jeans and sand between my toes. I can feel the vibrations of the subway car and taste salt on my tongue. It might be the ocean, or perhaps potato knish.

ALICE MORRIS

Because the Fox Crouches in the Street

because the fox crouches in the street, front leg cocked– I wait
as he fixes his eyes to mine, I look for fangs, for foaming mouth
he twitches his tail, tipped high
nothing else moves

as he fixes his eyes to mine, I look for fangs, for foaming mouth
no longer do I hear the rustling leaves, the birdlike chirps of squirrels
nothing else moves
I look for doors, the shortest line to run

no longer do I hear the rustling leaves, the birdlike chirps of squirrels
I have seen this fox before, have exposed his attempts at stealth
I look for doors, the shortest line to run
memories of a foxlike father arise, unbeckoned

I have seen this fox before, have exposed his attempts at stealth
the fox snarls, holds his ground
memories of a foxlike father arise, unbeckoned

I see the red/the disguise
the fox snarls, holds his ground
then breaks his stance, runs past homes where children play
I see the red/the disguise
later, when I ask, every child says no one has seen the fox

ALICE MORRIS

I Tried So Hard Not to Write This Donut Poem

Another temptation–
beware–
caution– stay away from the glazed *Krispy Kreme*– a gateway
donut, don't
even look at them, no– not
from a distance, and never as they arrive fresh off the truck– run–
go–
hightail it
immediately to the nearest
juice bar– think vitamin enriched
kale blended with
leafy dark greens, apples, strawberries, kiwi
maybe add mango, blueberries, banana, protein powder, but
never consider purchasing a half dozen gooey-ooy
over-the-top chocolate iced *kreme*-filled *Krispys*– not even for the
sake of
poetry–
quick– take my advice, get your feet into reverse
refuse to allow the devil's
sweet whispers
trick you into thinking the world of literature will suffer

until it gets its hands on your

very illuminating donut poem, and don't, for a second think that
your buff body

wishes– sacrificed to six *Krispy Kremes* ingested– for research– will
cause some

X factor to thrust

you and your donut poem into that great

Zen zone inhabited by the brightest, and the chubbiest of poet
masters.

LESLIE PIETRZYK

Something You're Proud Of

The room's what adults call tasteful, what I call blank. "Let's start with a list of accomplishments," the counselor says.

"Like I'm applying for college?" I ask. This is boring already. Secretly I'd hoped for one of those TV kid-shrinks with dolls and blocks and Play-Doh that tumble out of a fancy French amoire right when the session starts. Secretly I hoped for toys because that would be something I already know how handle. At fifteen, I know how to sprawl across a carpet, slipping mismatched plastic shoes on a ratty-haired Barbie and molding her a pink Play-Doh chair. The counselor could just watch me, a girl at play, as he scratches his notes onto a pad hidden in a gold-initialed leather portfolio, and at the end he'd go, "Aha. I've figured out what's wrong with you. This. This exactly."

And then I'd know.

I slouch deep into the couch, which is cloud-like and super-soft. I bet quarters drop from people's pockets into the cushion cracks. I ponder jamming my fingers down there surreptitiously.

He says, "It could be like a college application or it could just be something you're proud of. Does that make sense?"

I send my finest, hardest stare his way. My best friend, Jase, warned me that silence doesn't win. He said once he posed statue-still the entire fifty minutes uttering not one word, but the shrink told his mom it was a very productive session, and, Jase assured me, "A shrink wouldn't lie."

"Is this, like, for self-esteem?" I ask. "Because I think people think I think I'm too great. Like, that's more my problem, hyper self-esteem I think."

(Little snot. What makes you so special? My mother's voice at night.)

The counselor's got this red hair, kind of clownish and mildly distracting. Did my mom know when she booked me the appointment? Like, distracting me on purpose? He says, "No, not that. I guess I'd just like to hear you talk about yourself a bit, so we get to know each other."

"Is this a trap?" I laugh but I see in his pale blue eyes that he gets I'm serious.

"Is that what you think, I'm here to trap you?"

I slouch some more, till there's no deeper to slouch.

"Do you want to be here?" he asks. "Why do you think you're here?"

I say, "I'm really good at making cupcakes not from a mix. Like, really good." Of course I've never made cupcakes not from a mix. Where would I learn a stupid thing like that?

He's positively thrilled by what I've said, making me want to erase my words out of his mind. "Good!" He's talking like a daycare lady. "What else?"

"Well," I say. "Dogs really like me. Like on the street, they almost always come up to me before anyone else."

"Do you have a dog?"

"My mom won't let me."

A simple statement but saying "my mom" shatters the room. Like the molecules in the air bust apart. Cold starts up my toes and fingers. The thing about the dogs on the street is true,

BTW, and there I was, being real until I wrecked it all. I just had to mention my mom. Let me also erase those words.

He scribbles on a notepad, double-loops a circle with his pen.

Possibly I might cry. There's Kleenex like I'm supposed to.

"Is that what you mean?" I say. "I mean, is it an accomplishment that dogs like me? Dogs like everyone. I mean, I won't write that on a college app or whatever."

"Do you want a dog?" he asks.

"No," I say.

"What do you want, do you think," he asks. "Like, really want?"

I super-hate when adults like think they're talking like me.

"World peace," I say.

This silence. No ticking clock or water whooshing up pipes. My heart beats lightly in my ears. His stomach burbles, then mine. I imagine I'm hearing the rhythmic march of ants on the other side of the drywall.

The memory stuck in my head is of the last Christmas I believed in Santa Claus, writing a list for Santa, lined up to sit on mall-Santa's lap, grown-ups going, What do you want for Christmas? And suddenly it all seemed so stupid. Why would Santa give me anything? Why would anyone?

I say, "I didn't know I'm allowed to want something."

He sighs, his face wet-rag limp and as sad as I feel. I know I've said the exact wrong thing. I know I'm all wrong. Erase this whole day, please.

The Town Hall of Milton sits a block south of the Broadkill River. The town is named for the English poet, John Milton.

RUSSELL REECE

Last Dance:
Elegy for a Great Blue Heron

I try not to think of that white winter day
icy flakes hissed against the windows,
and across the river, you stood amidst
whirls of snow, under two sycamores,
branches crossed in a cathedral-like arch.

I try not to think of that white winter day
when through the snow-globe of my binoculars
I watched your hunched figure,
felt the heaviness of your beak.
You seemed to catch my eye for a moment,
then turned away, fluffed off a dusting of snow.

If only I could have done something old friend.
For years I admired your patience, your elegance,
your skill on the hunt. I felt blessed those evenings
the water was still, the night sounds had begun,
you'd glide across the river like a spirit.

So I try not to think of that white winter day
when wind howled through the eaves,

and as I got into bed your silhouette
huddled against the moonlit snow.

I woke to a brilliant sunrise. Ice gleamed
along the shoreline. Under the sycamores,
resting on an altar of drifted snow,
the blues and silvers of your lifeless body.
I try not to think of that white winter day.

Instead, I think of the spring morning
I watched you spread your wings
at the top of the tallest pine and dance.

RUSSELL REECE

Mambo

That day near Catoctin Mountain, in the valley covered with
snow,
I had to look twice to be sure.
You see, I've been accused of being fanciful
when it comes to sightings in the natural world.
But this time, there was no mistaking.

It was a mambo, I could tell
from the slide and the pause on the 2nd beat.
The proud oaks moved through their steps with poise and grace,
the cedars whirled in gowns of frosted crystal,
but it was the sycamores,
those tall lanky fellows with rhythm in their bones,
who really stole the show.

JOHN NEWLIN

Clean Up

When I was fifteen, my parents decided to pull me out of public school and send me to boarding school. I was an academic goof-off and sports fanatic, and they hoped a change would straighten me out. They could have chosen one of those updated, country-clubbish schools, the kind that has its own golf course or ski slope and fancy new dorms and classrooms. Instead, they picked a place that was both a monastery and a school. Porter Prep School was a collection of battered brick and beaverboard buildings set along a desolate New England coastline where the sun shines thirty days a year.

Because there was so little else to do, our time was filed with classes six days a week and tedious church services. The school chapel consisted of a low-ceilinged room, one the monks delighted filling with clouds of incense for even celebrations of the most obscure saint. During one service in honor of a St. Quintillus, first the fellow on my right, and then the guy on my left collapsed in heaps. Senior prefects arrived and yanked them out by the shoulders, shoes dragging across the linoleum, their bodies disappearing into the fog between my pew and the chapel door.

Had there not been an athletic program, I might have pulled out my toenails or drowned myself in the icy waters of the bay. The two-hour daily athletic period saved me. Still as bad a student as before, I did well on the soccer field and basketball court. By March of my junior year I'd started on both the soccer and basketball teams, and led the latter in scoring.

With spring vacation only days away, I was looking forward to playing first base and batting cleanup on the varsity baseball team. Basketball season over, I'd spent several hours throwing in the gym and hitting in the indoor batting cage.

The morning before vacation, we trekked up the hill to dining hall — the monks referred to it as the refectory — for our usual breakfast of watery scrambled eggs and rock-hard French toast. I'd drawn the assignment of being one of our table's waiters.

Breakfast ended, and I cleared while my partner trundled off to get a rag to wipe down the table. I dumped silverware into a metal milk pitcher, piled the dirty plates and coffee cups onto a tray, and headed off to the kitchen, imagining the homers I'd sock in April. Rounding the corner into the dishwashing area, I nearly collided with Hal McEvoy, our baseball coach, who was overseeing waiters.

"Whoa, Norton. What's the big rush?" He peered into the milk pitcher.

"What's this? Wasting precious milk? Think of how many people would die for a little milk. What in God's name were you thinking? You must be some kind of idiot."

Hmm. I was thinking I would get to go home for break in two days...and exactly how many people would starve because I'd wasted an eye-dropper's worth of milk?...maybe someone could use it to feed their cat?...was it okay to re-use milk that had been served to a table of high school kids?...could he please just let me go?

None of those responses seemed appropriate, so I stood there clutching the tray, tilting it inward as if fending him off. I was wondering when he'd tell me to be more careful the next time, or watch what I was doing, then shrug and let me pass. Instead, he lifted the pitcher off the tray, hoisted it into the air above my head, and turned it over as if performing a baptismal rite.

I was aware of the silverware raking my scalp, grazing my shoulders, one spoon catching in my jacket pocket, scoop side up like a tongue depressor. I felt my cheeks redden and my eyes water. Milk trickled into my hair, silently punctuating the clatter of knives, forks, and spoons rattling across the glazed tile.

Crimson-shaded thoughts danced in my head: how would I retaliate?

I'd make him regret his meanness. I wouldn't play baseball for him that spring. He'd be sorry…he'd lose his starting first baseman, his cleanup hitter. The team would lose all its games. I'd show him.

Coach McEvoy turned his back on me. I picked up the silver, deposited the now empty pitcher on the counter, hung up my waiter's jacket, the spoon still wedged in its pocket, and stalked toward my dorm.

Since athletics were required all three seasons, if I didn't play baseball, I'd have to do something. I'd played a lot of tennis, but my temper was so bad I'd quit the summer before. That left track. I'd ask the track coach, Fr. Anthony, if he needed a manager. He'd say yes. I wouldn't miss baseball. I could do some extra reading, maybe sing a solo for the glee club. And, who knows, Coach McEvoy might just apologize. If he did, I just might reconsider and play baseball.

He never did.

SHERRY CHAPPELLE

Take Me Home

At Safe Harbor Healthcare
it's a gritty-grey November afternoon.
        Our upbeat baker's dozen of a cappella
breaches the jetty to bring our brand of upbeat, jazzy.
        From smiles and cheers and come back soon
in the light-bright parlor of Assisted Living,
        we slip through a hyphen hallway
into Memory Care.

        The door clicks behind us.
 Shut, it is a *trompe l'oeil* bookcase.
        Hostages here, we launch our set
with "Goody, Goody" — to silent stares
        heads on tables and then
at "Take Me Home" we hear the screams:
        stop that racket noise-noise-noise
                SHUT UP.

        Pitch dropped and lyrics lost
we are untethered
        swept away
in a rip current
        before the final lines
        or harmony
        pulls us in.

SHERRY CHAPPELLE

Mill Town

Strong place, queen city, once
the mansions on the hill ruled Water Street,
White and Church. Men with pocket watches
walked to Railroad Square. Now nursing homes slump,
fill with what was once thought upper crust. Offices
of small-town lawyers sell attics filled with old fur coats
and trundle beds, and advertise a port-cochere.

Rubber rumbles over the chink-clink bridge,
another U-Haul packed. In the rear view only red and grift,
the blistered shells of cars and crusted men
in DD's parking lot. They clasp their Buds and grumble
from their worn lawn chairs, betray
that honest work they shared, of uppers and lowers,
of heels and soles, before the jobs went south.

Two battered boys drift from all they know.
Almost-men, fed all their lives from a freezer or a tin,
they've watched their world grind small, seen
river's edge grow tire necklaces, and condoms sprout.
Sludge rules the bank where a poet wrote of barefoot boys
and novelists mined dreams deferred. Now in a land of fallen
ceilings, tattooed girls, four o'clock Mass, deflowered altar
boys, they visit Jimmy's Market for news and bread and a ticket
out of town. They cross the membrane from where they've been

to somewhere they think they want to be. Under
the bridge's rusty span, a fingernail moon reflects.
Over it they drag their lives like a string of cans.

MEMORY

The rain tapped, knocked against the hood, as if begging to be let in. Morgan's grip on the steering wheel tightened. What if Abigail were here? He patted the sonogram photo in his pocket as he shifted in his seat and exhaled. The stench of cigarettes wafted through the stagnant air as he listened to passing cars glide across the slick road. The sun had set, the city long since knowing the light of day. He watched a bright hotel sign with a picture of a sunrise flash repetitively, sending some unknown signal to him and him alone.

Abigail was out there somewhere living a perfectly normal life, no doubt forgetting the depth of the feelings she once had, even if the divorce had resulted in screaming matches. Morgan was against it from the start, but he didn't protest. He deserved it. Like a moth to flame, he knew Abigail was drawn to divorce, believing that there was something better for her. It was the stillborn death of daughter that reminded her that death is permanent and she had no time to waste on a man like Morgan.

The rain picked up, the noise snapping Morgan out of his thoughts. He had spent the last three hours at a diner forty-five minutes from home, hoping the distance would provide space for reflection, without running into someone he knew. Now, three cups of coffee and a plate of dry eggs later, he sat in the car Abigail let him have, probably, he thought, to distance herself from the memories of driving back and forth to the hospital. He rested his forehead against the worn steering wheel, and closed his eyes. Suddenly, he could see his daughter dancing in sunflower fields, her black hair, like her mother's, catching the breeze. Her pale skin blossomed as blood rushed through her tiny body as her feet hopped across freshly cut grass. Moments later, he opened his eyes and the dream ended.

He wondered how Abigail's palms were always so smooth.

December was a cruel month. The death of nature, mixed with the lively spirit of the season and well-wishers, was a specific type of torture. Morgan imagined Abigail gift shopping with her sister, able to trudge on after their daughter's death. Life keeps going, she would remind him while she was getting ready for work and he was still in bed. He wondered if she harbored a secret sadness, one of great depth and only her outward appearance was "normal."

Sleep lapped at Morgan in a steady current. His thoughts began to morph into a creature all their own, a dangerous beast encompassing good and evil. His thoughts reached a surreal, bone shattering density. Exhausted, his eyes finally closed in sleep.

When he awoke, a goat was pressing its cloven hoof into his side.

"Are you alright?" the goat said.

Morgan's eyes shot open wide.

It couldn't possibly be, yet he could see the goat's course brown and white hair.

"Who are you?" He realized he meant what, not who.

"I'm a simple goat. That's all. I'm flesh and bone, just like you."

It didn't explain much, but in every sense, it was a goat: a talking goat.

"Who lives here?"

"People like me and you."

Morgan took a moment to survey the surroundings. There were buildings overgrown with roots and weeds; black and red beams sprouting from the bases. Nearby was a large pond. He noticed, raccoons, bird, and wondered if they had the ability to speak. In the distance, a girl in a short dress frolicked in the fields, her black hair glistening.

"What kind of place is this?"

"This is a place where anyone can live. For some, it is Heaven. For others, it is Hell." The goat paused, turning to make eye contact with Morgan.

"Which is it for you?"

"I… don't know."

"Of course you don't know. Not yet, at least."

The goat's tone sounded almost threatening.

`"How long will I be here?"

"You ask a lot of questions. Some leave after only minutes. Some have never left."

Morgan looked back. The young girl was gone.

The goat's ears twitched. "Explore. I'm easy to find if you need me."

The goat hopped away.

Morgan looked at the sky and thought of Abigail's blue, blue veins. What would she do? He was sure she would explore and find a way to escape.

But did he want to leave?

Though desolate, the place seemed more peaceful than the city. But, if he stayed he needed to get to know the place. Some buildings stood taller than others, with staircases and walls still standing. He walked toward the building with the highest staircase. From the remains, the building appeared to have been an office building or apartments. As he walked, chunks of drywall clapped against wood creating chalky clouds. The staircase was missing boards, but for some reason, he felt no fear,

At the third floor, there was a hole, blocking his path. On the wall, there were photographs of Abigail and him. He patted his pocket. The sonogram was still there.

He turned when he heard feet clopping up the steps. It was the goat

"Is this what you wanted?" he asked, in a calm voice.

"No. It's not."

"The paused. "Look," the goat said, "the animals are playing a game."

Morgan looked through a large hole in the floor to the ground.

Sheep were in a circle; all sitting except one, who held a dark, blocky object between his front hooves.

A gun?

"Wait, what are they doing?"

"It's just a game," the goat said.

The gun was passed around, with each member of the circle. The sheep that was standing held the gun to its head and pulled the trigger. Morgan's blood ran cold.

Morgan glanced at the goat, but neither spoke.

A shot rang out. Morgan fell through the hole in the floor, knowing that within seconds he would be dead or injured.

Hours later, he awoke on the floor of his apartment. He was drenched in sweat; his arms and legs were relaxed. He patted his pocket. The sonogram was bent.

As sunlight filtered through the curtains, Morgan rose from the floor. Images of a goat and sheep and gun flashed in his head, but he pushed them aside. He opened the curtains and smiled. For the first time in years, he felt alive.

LARRY KELTS

Rumbles & Reason Out of the North

for Mikki & Michael

Rumors of unlicensed shop keepers
massing near the border trickled into the Park.

Once, in London, we too were out
for a day without a licensed guide.

A Park was but a dream back then
& there, but rumors stirred it up.

The sun's script, bright & real, read now & then, lit the way:
That day we visited Marx's grave in Highgate.

The tomb (death of the body, material & base
of all that's real) was strewn with flowers,

acolytes dressed in black surrounded
the monument & massive head that still

supports & funds economic carnivals
(like this Water Park) that promise to bury

the invisible hand that pointed us to
our next destination, Down House &

Darwin's Gardens. The patchwork belies
another grand narrative (of heart & spirit)

rising into its own to archive
mise-en-scene of desire & play out survival.

The rumbles continue stronger with each passing
night, & it is this delving into soul-stuff

that sends me back to the third stop of that
long-ago day in London:

Freud's House & Museum.
Vera Frankel's Body Missing exhibition

presented a vast bounty of Art stolen & missing,
as traders from the North creep closer.

But back at Freud's (he, of course, also,
an architect of mind & completing

this tripartite tour) where the infamous couch
remains & we take a turn reclining

on this token of a dying vision that returns
to the Park & what is replayed as the past.
The British, like you, drop now only to express
a need for entertainment & to stuff

satchels with souvenirs & mementos
of a lost culture that we must resurface to

understand what we lose & find of ourselves,
remembering that day in London where,

with dream intoxicated minds, we reasoned the past,
& strolled, high on enlightenment, toward this Park.

LARRY KELTS

Twisted Hair

I was having a bad hair day when they spilled out of the mountains & ate our roots & crisped fish. When they began to eat our dogs I knew they had to be stopped. Their hair colors were fabulous, but they refused to reveal their hairdresser. Later, we agreed to watch their horses, then we helped them build boats, & sent them on their scripted way.

When they returned the following Spring, dreams began to disappear & signs of our Nez Perce past began to vanish along twisted trails. The hairpin turns they insisted on taking nearly cost them a season of delay. At the races, they followed our flying hair, but never caught our train. Their renderings remained twisted compared to our straight-out translations. Some of their horses refused to return, or travel their twisted course over the snow-covered mountains. When we complained, they set up an Urgent Care Center to treat our most common maladies: sore eyes & muscles. They put drops in our eyes & soaked our muscles, then they straightened our hair, but it was my twisted hair that had propelled me to power, so I threatened to send them down the straight & narrow if they continued jerking our locks.

We beat them in Spring training base(ball) & they combed their hair & left before the regular season. Sometimes, even when you know you're right & know no matter how twisted the reasoning might be you still give in & let others dictate the terms & carry off the spoils. Personally I, Twisted Hair, think we shouldn't have listened to the old woman. We should have scalped them & twisted their hair & hung their severed heads from a pole, but it's too late & here we remain waiting for the next group of tourists to look upon us without the least bit of fear we once inspired.

JENNIFER MORRELL

The Sky Flipped Upside Down

I booked a flight to Arizona to see Brad, a guy I'd met through mountain biking. We had become inseparable in short measure, riding and hanging out at every opportunity. I felt that charge you get at the beginning, the kind that obviates sleep, the kind that makes your skin spark. But a few months in, he had returned west, to a land I'd seen only in movies and that carried, in my mind, a profound romanticism. A year later, I was spending a month's pay on airfare. I would fly to see Brad, then hop a plane to Colorado to visit an aunt and uncle.

I took a big plane from Baltimore to Phoenix, then waited ten hours for my connecting flight to Flagstaff. The layover was supposed to be about an hour, but the plane we were to board had mechanical issues. As plane after plane took off and the departures area emptied, a handful of us remained, scooting closer, making jokes about our luck. When we finally boarded, the motley lot of us had coalesced into a tribe. The gentle giant of our group was a mechanic for small aircraft like the one we were boarding. During our day-long holdup at the gate, he had confided how fearful he was to fly in the very planes he fixes. "You cannot imagine the shit that goes wrong with these things," he had said.

I was nervous when the plane landed, but not about the aircraft; I was nervous to see Brad after a year apart. It was dark when we emerged from the regional airport and walked to his car—a Jeep, dusty and aged, with nary a top, just a bit of fabric stretched like a drum cover across the overhead center bars. The flapping fabric and the whooshing air as we hurtled down the highway were as loud as drums. And it was cold. So cold that I sat confused, almost angry, at how cold I was. I'd just flown across the country to see about a boy, so I should have been feeling cared for, not so chilled my fingers were growing numb. In the silence between us, enforced by the deafening noise overhead, I leaned my head back and beheld the desert as we drove east. As soon as we were clear of Flagstaff, all the tall stuff—buildings, trees—fell away, and the world on either side of the interstate was flat and seemingly infinite, like the sky flipped upside down.

Brad's apartment was garage space in a boxy metal building designated as the town's recreation center, where he was serving as the activities director. One wall was a working overhead door. A daybed, a couch, a small table and chairs were the only furnishings, and the patch of gray carpet did nothing to assuage the industrial feel of the room.

Although we seemed united in our expectation of picking up where we'd left off, something felt the slightest bit askew right away. Lights out, I crawled into bed alongside my cowboy and waited for the rodeo. What followed was more rote than romantic.

Brad was scheduled to work for the first day or two, but he loaned me his car. The directions to get to major sights were as simple as sunshine: Go west on I40 until you get to Meteor Crater; go east on I40 until you get to the Petrified Forest. I drove around in that skeletal Jeep, bumping along the highway, thrilled as I'd ever been in my life: a hand on the gear shift, a hand on the wheel, and my eyes absorbing a land as foreign to me as the surface of the moon. I felt as if I was wide-awake and dreaming all at once. Despite anything happening, or not, in the daybed in the garage I was happy: this was what living was all about. I felt galaxies away from my desk in Delaware. I knew, upon return, those office walls would be transparent, the rest of the world beckoning.

One evening, Brad said he had the next two days off and suggested I choose between mountain biking in The Peaks or backpacking overnight at the Grand Canyon. I chose the Grand Canyon, and we spent the rest of the night provisioning our hiking packs. We got a late start the following morning, and by the time we reached the Grand Canyon, it was verging on mid-afternoon. More important, he'd had a sudden realization on the ride there: He did have to work the next day, so we could only hike down a short way, then back up and head home that same night. The rest of the drive, I vacillated between incredulity and disgust. How did he not envision this problem while we were sitting on the concrete floor packing our gear? What kind of person is capable of planning and preparing for a two-day overnight hike in the Grand Canyon without realizing he's scheduled instead to run a softball tournament he had organized?

With only a few hours of daylight left in which to hike the canyon trail before the deep afternoon shadows would overtake us, we couldn't park the car fast enough once at the trailhead lot. To Brad's consternation, I hustled to the port-a-potty to unload the loose contents of my bowels, which left my body shaky. I leaned against the Jeep as he pulled the various backpack straps across his hips, waist, chest — Clip, Clip, Clip. Ready to go?

I watched him, the cowboy, stride confidently ahead while I carefully picked my way down the steep slope, a combination of thick orange powder and loose rocks of the same color. My legs wobbled, and I sweated with more than effort, by then convinced I had a fever. But we made it to the first flat viewing area. For years, I kept a picture of him standing there, hands on hips, taking in the view. I had snapped the picture with my disposable camera while I rested behind him on a rock as large as a sofa. I could just run up and push him off, I remember thinking when I clicked the button.

The next day I sat in sweltering sun and watched softball for hours. By then, even though I was sleeping alone on the couch, Brad continued to play host, facilitating a day trip that will never fade from my mind. We drove out to private property with a woman of Native American descent. She took us across a stretch of dry land beyond a large metal gate. We hiked until we came to a gash in the ground, which turned out to be a small canyon. One at a time, we descended a series of metal steps and handholds into a world you'd never guess existed from the thirsty, tumbleweed land above. They said we'd see rock art, but I saw none. Just high rocky walls and a slight ribbon of water snaking around a bend. Look closer, she said, gesturing. She was pointing to a picture that, once in focus, startled me with delight. Ancient drawings and carvings adorned the walls around us. The promised rock art was everywhere.

One of Brad's friends took us to the community pool one night and horseback riding the next day. I was grateful for the hospitality, but I knew things were souring with Brad. I called the airline about an earlier flight to Colorado, but everything was booked.

I asked Brad to drop me off at a youth hostel in Flagstaff — a full three days before my flight. Once there, alone, panic shot through me. From a pay phone, I sought sympathy from my mom. Buck up, she advised. Rent a car and go do stuff. So, I did. I ate fantastic food from healthy eateries unlike anything we had back home. I shared an outdoor table with a woman who turned out to be a tarot card reader. I was too cheap — or too spineless, or too skeptical — to pay for a reading, but I talked to her while I sipped coffee. When it rained, I drove down the street to see a movie, Phenomenon, with John Travolta. The soundtrack will forever transport me right back to that table, that coffee, that card-turning woman—particularly Eric Clapton's "Change the World," the lyrics synonymous with one of my life's tectonic shifts.

When the sun shone, I drove south to Red Rocks State Park. Bouncing foolishly uphill along a rutted dirt road, I wondered whether I was headed for certain danger. At the top, I saw with relief that other cars had managed the trek. Although boulders and bumpy rock walls abounded, there was no clear view of anything from where I stood when I exited the car. I walked nearer to others, turned my head, and was struck by the view and our elevation. We stood atop a ledge, the fiery landscape tumbling hundreds of feet below us. I have to pee, I realized with alarm. Behind a rock jutting out of the ground toward the sky like a fist, I squatted. As I yanked my shorts back up, I laughed out loud at the wonder of it all—of everything, really.

My aunt and uncle picked me up in Gunnison. They drove me to their log house, which sits a smart distance from the town of Crested Butte. From their elevation, the town at night is a small square, as lit up and inviting as a Christmas tree. They offered me a bike one day, and I headed out in the direction they advised. Eventually, they said, you'll come to Emerald Lake. It was clear how the lake got its name. It was the kind of lake a kid would draw, picking the brightest green-blue crayon in the box. I pictured the pond near my childhood home, its water dark, murky. They make a crayon for that too: brown.

Back at the house, I shared a bedroom with a cayenne pepper plant. It sat in a pot on top of a dresser, surprising me when I first took notice. I'd never seen a plant of that kind, its perfectly red, tiny fruit sprinkled evenly throughout its branches. Someday, I vowed, I'd be the sort of person who grows a cayenne pepper plant in her house.

Since I had first touched down in Arizona, the land had left me spellbound. The west was so different from where I'd spent my life. The vistas were wider than I knew possible, wide enough to imagine a spherical curve on either side, wide enough to help me see beyond my lament: The world's too big to rue one cowboy. For the first time, I grasped that I was on a rocky planet, covered with landscapes exquisitely varied and cruising through the cosmos, catching the occasional meteor on the chin like a prizefighter. The immense reaches of it all made me feel small in the best possible way. If plans turned belly up in the future, I'd have this trip, this new knowledge of just how much there is out there, to lean on. I'm a tiny stitch on an ocean-sized quilt: one stitch, but a part of something grand. That thought is a buoy. Pay attention to the wide vistas, the west whispered, and you'll never forget your place.

GEMELLE JOHN

If You Count

There are several ways to be a beating heart and still feel everything a daybreak

A moon and cool flesh raging at 3 am fecund and alone you are always the shell

is there anyone waiting for us in this pain will I find you there still gnawing your anguish

does that make you human or now how can I love you myself a siren groaning

into hand towels every morning still living like everything is happening and none of it is us

why flesh between our shoulder blades why heavy and no cross and nothing fully blistered

and then we are the blood made glass watching and becoming a reason to love

someone you've only ached for heart

you do not belong here

GEMELLE JOHN

If Grief Plural

In the third grade there is no spectrum for death/ Only the gnawing and how to draw it into three days more/ so our eyes glaze as plumes of smoke dress the skyline/ we observe it with a modesty painted onto the outer boroughs/ from the time we are born/ brown and one more /our hearts are taught to absorb adequately/ So on this day/ chaos a liaison for our grief/ we watch *The Land Before Time* in unpressed plaid uniforms/ eat what's left of the pizza Pringles/ First 30 then 17 then 5 /students remain/ parents come to clutch the/ only thing they own/ students refract a century's worth of news with every question/ the newspapers know new deaths by the hour/ that aren't ours/this time/ this outside/ might be home/ but in the outer boroughs/ unless it's burning/ it probably isn't ours/so to this day/ simmer has always been an answer/ when people ask where we were / I say invisible, choking, and still a ritual unburied

JEAN YOUKERS

Elegy for My Dad

I miss the Dad of my childhood,
who taught me to ride a bike,
who whistled when vaulting down the stairs,
prepared to teach in suits and wingtip shoes
I miss the Dad who whisked us off to Florida in summer,
who bought a pet Capuchin monkey there,
who came home and built a cage
with painted palm trees the monkey tried to climb
the Dad who told funny stories,
made up new "old sayings,"
tried to do magic tricks   but smashed plates instead —
I miss him, too
I miss the Dad of my youth
who soothed my adolescent angst,
who could always make me laugh
(except when he taught me to drive)
the Dad of later years
stayed up late to talk,
made falling on his head sound like
a new way of dismounting his bike
I miss the Dad who, even after Mom was gone
and he was blind,

listened to talking books,
eager to learn — the teacher, ever the student
I miss my Dad
and always will,
I still hear his laughter

JEAN YOUKERS

Grandma's Apprentice

When I smell lilacs I'm transported back to Grandma's house, where she is wearing her printed housedress and apron and stretching to hang sheets. My job is handing her clothespins. Stiff and wooden, they look like little people with no arms and tiny round heads. The cat, Sunshine, brushes by, whining. I reach down, smoothing his silken yellow hair. Toby, the dog, is observing us from his post on the porch. When all the sheets are hung there is a wall of whiteness and the smell of Clorox overpowers the lilacs. "One more," Grandma says, and we carry the empty basket into the cool basement to retrieve another load from the round white wringer washer.

Slaughter Beach was founded in 1681. Does the name derive from the many horseshoe crabs who die on its beaches when they come to spawn in the spring? Or is it based on the slaughter of peace-seeking native Americans in the late 1600s?

CHRISTINA DURBOROW

Nunzi's Peccadilloes

When I was in my 20s, the magnitude of having only one living grandparent hit me. I never met my father's father, and Dad's mother was in a nursing home for most of my childhood.

My maternal grandparents, Mom-Mom and Pops, loomed large in my memories, but I could only remember them as they looked when I last saw them. According to my recollection, they had always looked the same: old. Perhaps it's a function of growing older myself, but my definition of "old" has become increasingly fluid over the last two decades, and now when I see pictures of the two of them from my childhood birthday parties, they appear much younger and livelier than I remember, proving my memory to be hopelessly unreliable.

Mom-Mom and Pops had lived in a red brick rancher with three tiers of gardens surrounding the property. The front door was purely ornamental. When entering through the back porch, visitors immediately were greeted by the permeating smell of basil and garlic as they made their way into the kitchen, where my big Italian family gathered every Sunday for dinner.

Mom-Mom was the first person my cousins and I ran to for comfort when we shoved too many pumpkin seeds up our noses or wound up with rulers stuck down our throats. But beleaguered by many years of child bearing and housekeeping, my grandmother could find no comfort of her own. What she needed was a good cry, but having no tears left, she stood at the kitchen window every morning with a pocket mirror and a bottle of artificial tears. Her day began drawing to a close once the dinner dishes were washed and she settled in on the couch for an evening with The Golden Girls or Angela Lansbury.

Mom-Mom, always a heavy smoker, had several heart attacks and mini-strokes before she died at the age of 62. The sixth heart attack killed her. Pops lived on for a decade or so, at first in the house the two of them had shared. But once he started falling and couldn't get up on his own, my aunts and uncles sat him down and broke the news: time to consider assisted living. Instead, Pops sold his house and lived like a nomad, spending a few months at a time in the home of whichever one of his grown children was willing to have him and moving on once he'd worn out his welcome.

Because my grandfather was not one to sit quietly and mind his own business, the arrangement was not ideal. A new interest in cooking had him filling freezers with lunchmeat and sausage to make stromboli for everyone he knew in the tri-state area. His culinary passion took us by surprise—he never cooked when my grandmother was alive—and he commandeered kitchens for days at a time. Because he slept in a recliner in front of the TV, living rooms became bedrooms, which meant multiple rooms in each house lost significant functionality. I'm not sure which of my mother's siblings put a foot down first, but after a few years, with nowhere left to go, Pops reluctantly got his own place in a retirement community.

Not long after he moved in, I began an earnest attempt not just to learn our family's history, but also to acquire some of my grandfather's recipes—I wanted his legacy to live on through his pasta e fagioli.

"Will you teach me how to make meatballs and tell me the story of how you met and fell in love with Mom-Mom?" I asked. He readily agreed.

On my way to his place a few days later, I thought about the glamorous wedding portrait that had hung on my grandmother's wall. Mom-Mom and Pops looked like Ava Gardner and Frank Sinatra. My grandmother stood proudly, ebony hair perfectly curled and coifed, dark eyes glittering. Dapper in his rumpled tux, my grandfather stood behind her, hair carelessly tousled, eyes and lips hinting at both the mischief and the promise of youth.

When I got to my grandfather's apartment, he pulled two huge bags of meatballs out of the freezer. Maybe the meatball-making mission had been foiled, but I was still committed to my fact-finding pursuit. Pops shoved a couple of Banquet frozen dinners into the microwave for lunch, and over Salisbury steak, he talked while I took diligent notes.

I knew he'd been shot in the stomach and left for dead when he was a young gas station owner. And I knew that was why he slept in a recliner instead of a bed and why he walked hunched over long before he hit 60. But I hadn't known there was only $2.38 in the register at the time of the robbery.

"You might be interested to know, cara mia," he said, "that your grandmother and I were from the same town in Italy—Bogatta—but we didn't meet until years later when we were both living in South Philly. I knew right away that I wanted to propose and soon figured out a way to do it with style.

"After a few dates," he continued, with a sly smile on his lips, "I sneaked into your grandmother's house in the middle of the night and serenaded her with the help of a five-piece swing band. After the nuptials, your grandmother worked at Curtis

Publices and smuggled pints of Great River Whiskey home in her garter belt."

Soon the day of storytelling turned into night, and my grandfather tossed two more frozen dinners into the microwave—fried chicken this time. After we had our fill of eating and talking, we watched Jeopardy and Wheel of Fortune before he sent me on my way with two giant bags of frozen meatballs.

My grandfather suffered continuing complications from the gunshot wound, and years of smoking finally caught up with him. He got sick shortly after my visit—pneumonia had infected his weakened lungs—and he spent weeks on end in the hospital with only brief interludes back at his apartment. When my he died, we had said our good-byes many times, and his passing was almost a relief. Although I was disappointed that I didn't know how to make a decent meatball, I was grateful to have had that day with him and grateful that he was no longer suffering. And having never really recovered from my grandmother's death, his later years were dominated by an intense longing to see her again. He went peacefully, surrounded by family and his parish priest, believing he would join his beloved wife on the other side.

If I had been born into a different family, this is where the story would end. A few years after my grandfather's death, however, my sister was in Italy looking for the town where my grandparents were born. Did extended family live there? Was she able to track down any long-lost relatives we could reunite with? Not quite. My sister's search for Bogatta had turned into a wild goose chase, as I found out when she called from overseas.

"What's the name of that town Pops told you about? The one where he and Mom-Mom came from?"

"It's called Bogatta. I think it's spelled B-O-G-A-T-T-A."

"Yeah. That's not a place."

"What do you mean that's not a place?"

"I can't find it on a map. And whenever I ask about it, people shake their heads at me in confusion. Can you double-check what he said to you?"

I ran downstairs to find my notebook while my sister held the line. I definitely had written Bogatta. Maybe I got it wrong somehow? I was certain I had confirmed the spelling with my grandfather at least three times.

It was time to call Aunt Grace, my grandfather's sister, who was a character in her own right. She dressed in cheerful hot pink and bright aqua blue and carried a teeny tiny dog named Rusty in her purse long before it was fashionable to do so. Her perennial smile and welcoming face softened the edges of her no-nonsense worldview. She was also a great clarifier when it came to my grandfather—it was she, for instance, who informed us in her husky smoker's voice that what my grandfather called a stromboli was in reality a calzone. Aunt Grace set us straight on Bogatta as well.

"Your grandfather was full of shit. Your grandparents were not from the same small town in Italy," she said, "and neither of the towns their families were from were called Bogatta."

"What about the other stuff," I asked, "the proposal, the serenade, the swing band?"

"Never happened," Aunt Grace said with finality.

I felt foolish for believing my grandfather's stories and wondered how I never had known what a big fat liar he was.

After some time passed, though, I realized I never recognized my grandfather's capacity for invention because I hadn't wanted to. His tall tales had started in my childhood when I found an old metal barrel in the woods behind the house. I realize now it was just an empty keg discarded by drunken teenagers. But back then, I believed my grandfather when he declared it must have been left behind by the Vikings who used to live in those woods. I dragged numerous cousins and friends up the hill and through the trees to excitedly show them that Nordic relic.

Can I blame my grandfather for coming up with new stories to peak my interest—fictitious family secrets and the invented shenanigans of a time when he was younger and more carefree? Then again, not everything he said was a lie. As far as I know, those gas station robbers really did walk away with a measly $2.38.

Before our day of storytelling, I remembered my grandparents largely as they looked and acted in their twilight years. Mom-Mom shuffling through the house in a red floral housecoat, reading glasses around her neck, chipped red nail polish revealing thick yellow smoker's nails as she reached for the percolator. Pops hunched in his recliner, old gray trousers belted well above his natural waistline and worn brown moccasins beneath the lounge chair.

My grandfather's stories, whether true or false, were a gift because they expanded the catalogue of images in my mind. The wedding portrait of my grandparents will always enchant me. The portrait now hangs in my living room. And even though it probably never happened, I like to imagine my grandmother, laughing as she tucks a pint of Great River Whiskey into her garter belt before sashaying out of the distillery.

LESLIE SYSKO

Battledore

The sun opens its mouth
to night, setting a curving

river aflame. You're there
swinging evening's pendulum.

It's ancient, your pounding—
battledore bearing down,

cloth heap dull and sodden,
body black, bending

like a tree rebuked by storm.
Stay your battledore, hold

your metronome silent.
Where river's fire burns darkest,

deeper than blue herons' careful
wading, you'll see reflections

shimmering: axman
striking, baseballer batting,

savage hunting, protester
picketing, politician

pontificating, striver
striving — .

History's insistent ones.
Did you see them? Were they

men? One epoch after
another, embattled

archetypes fledged against
you, snarling your mind's

gnarled roots, trapping you
shoal-shallow, even you —

you pugilist timekeeper.
You've pummeled a low

bassline for history's
winged thrash.

16

The insects making so much noise
in August were silent in June.

July's sweet cha cha cha
trills as though they're tentative,

trying their music before
they really need it.

August burgeons
with puberty's coming.

Suddenly they deafen the world
to everything else — wild, deep,

striving, locked together,
mouths open, legs humid,

sticky, rubbing against each other,
arms clinging fast to the rocking bark,

eyes closed in rapture like Odysseus
lashed to the mast, straining,

already ruined, begging for more.

On Hearing My Son Was Socrates and My Husband Frank Sinatra

My son dresses in blue sailor suits. His choice, not mine. The red cowboy boots are his choice, too. Along with the quizzical look on his face.

"Mommy, why can't we see air?"

Not another question. Not now. You know how it is. You're hoping for an ordinary day. The kind of day you read about in all those Parenting Done Right books. Not you. Not today. Not any day.

Mommy, why can't we see air?"

Your husband, Paul, looks across the breakfast table at Sean, then you. Inquisitiveness is a sign of genius. Paul's smiling when he says this and your lips quiver involuntarily. You don't mention the other three-year-old with autism, the one on the TV last night. It's all too much, even for you. You wonder if the little boy will turn out okay, and if his father thinks he's a genius, too.

"Answer him," Paul says, and his smile widens.

You begin to hate his smile. You begin to hate yourself for not saying what you're thinking about saying. You tried once, only once. You still remember how your vowels overran your consonants and you turned into a Valley Girl from one of those Molly Ringwald movies when Paul smiled, and you wondered why you ever married a prick like him in the first place. Oh yeah, you remind yourself, you were nineteen and pregnant, that's why.

"Mommy, why can't we see air?"

Please stop. But you adore Sean and refocus, as if repeating the question is just what your bone-tired brain needs to re-energize. Besides, didn't Socrates say we learn more from questions than answers? Maybe—just maybe—Sean's autism serves a useful purpose. This you could live with.

You wave a Pop Tart and glance at Paul for help. Nothing. Men are just different you tell yourself and you're surprised how much you sound like your mother when you say it.

You could give up, but you long to feel Paul's tongue slide across your cheek like he has to have you right there and now. You see the way he watches your neighbor with the tiny waist and big boobs. You wonder if he's sliding his tongue across her cheek, and if he is, if he's fucking her with that grunting sound that lets you know a part of him is becoming a part of you.

Shush, you tell yourself. Paul is Sean's father and your love revolves around them like the earth revolves around the sun. This is why you won't mention that you imagined seeing him with the neighbor at the mall right before Sean ran off. Or that a whole hour had passed before a security guard found him in the parking lot dissecting a telescope and eating fudge. No, you won't tell Paul any of this. You know there's no point.

"Mommy, why can't we see air?"

"I'm still thinking." Paul leaves the table as you speak.

A few minutes later, you and Sean drive back to the mall. Somehow, in between the telescope and the fudge, he pocketed Superman and you need to pay for him. As you break for a shift in traffic, it suddenly occurs to you that everything is made of atoms and molecules, so air is made of atoms and molecules. Stay calm, you remind yourself. You can explain that atoms and molecules are microscopic, then explain microscopic and give so many examples you'll be home before Sean can ask another question you can't answer.

"MOMMY, WHY CAN'T WE SEE AIR?

You carry Sean inside Macy's. He is screaming. The cashier stares at you, and you hold Sean closer. On the way home, he repeats the question and you attempt to answer, but each time he demands a shorter more concise answer and kicks the seat.

You are relieved when you finally get home. Paul is smiling, of course. You hand Sean over and watch Paul deposit him on the sofa and pat his head. You are about to speak, but through the window you catch a glimpse of the neighbor woman looking your way, and you choke on your words

"What's wrong now?" Paul snaps. "You aren't happy if you don't have something to worry about."

It's a lie. But, you don't say anything. Paul is too loud to listen. Just this morning you awoke to Frank Sinatra, not the real one — rather your semi-nude wannabe belting out "My Way," as if your bedroom was Carnegie Hall, and a packed house was hanging onto his every note. His eyes were telling you not to interrupt, so you didn't. Instead, you gathered Sean, and as you expected, as the day progressed, things only got worse. Still, you kept moving. Not forward. Just moving.

The Candlelight Theater of Arden has produced a broad spectrum of theatrical performances for more than 75 years, and is supported by the Delaware Division of the Arts and the National Endowment for the Arts.

Contributing Writers and Poets

Sarah Barnett is vice president of the Rehoboth Beach Writers Guild and enjoys leading Free Writes, teaching writing classes, and composing essays and short fiction while walking her dog on the beach. Her work has appeared in *Delmarva Review*, *Delaware Beach Life* and other publications. Before retiring to Delaware and discovering the joys of writing creatively, she had careers as teacher, librarian, and lawyer.

Sandra Beasley is the author of three poetry collections—*Count the Waves*, *I Was the Jukebox*, and *Theories of Falling*—as well as *Don't Kill the Birthday Girl: Tales from an Allergic Life*. She served as the editor for *Vinegar* and *Char: Verse from the Southern Foodways Alliance*. Honors for her work include the 2019 Munster Literature Centre's John Montague International Poetry Fellowship, a 2015 NEA fellowship, and four DC Commission on the Arts and Humanities fellowships. She lives in Washington, D.C., and teaches with the University of Tampa low-residency MFA program.

Sherry Chappelle finds wonder in all seasons at the edge of the Atlantic in Rehoboth Beach. A former teacher, she won the 2011 Dogfish Head Poetry Prize for *Salmagundi*. In 2016, she was named Emerging Artist in Poetry by the Delaware Division of the Arts. Her work has appeared in numerous anthologies and publications and been nominated for the Pushcart Prize

Melanie Czerwinski is a graduate of the University of Delaware. Her work has been published or is forthcoming in *The Sucarnochee Review, Dark Ink Press, From Whispers To Roars, Not Your Mother's Breast Milk, Underwood Press, Reflex Fiction, littledeathlit,* and *X-R-A-Y Literary Magazine.*

Christina Durborow is new to the Delaware writing scene but a veteran instructor of literature and academic writing in the greater Philadelphia region. She writes about food, wine, family, the perils of the 1990s and coming-of-age in small-town America. She lives in Wilmington, Delaware, with her dear and loving husband.

Irene Fick's second collection of poetry, *The Wild Side of the Window* (2018), was published by Main Street Rag. Her first book, *The Stories We Tell* (The Broadkill Press), received first place awards from the National Federation of Press Women and the Delaware Press Association. Her poems have been published in five anthologies and in such journals as *Poet Lore*, Gargoyle, *The Broadkill Review, Philadelphia Stories, Mojave River Review,* and *Pittsburgh Poetry Review.* She is a Pushcart nominee for her poem, "We Didn't Know Anything," published in Poet Lore. In 2018, she participated in the annual Bread Loaf Writers' Conference in Vermont. She lives in Lewes, Delaware and is active in the Rehoboth Beach Writers' Guild and Coastal Writers.

Karen Hurley-Heyman, a 2019 Delaware Division of the Arts Fellow in Literature (emerging poet category), earned her Ph.D. in Dramatic Art at UC Berkeley. In San Francisco, she developed a theater career before moving in 2000, to join the UD theater faculty. She was later hired as Director of the Delaware Institute for Arts in Education and Delaware Wolf Trap and worked with Head Start Programs and K-12 classes throughout Delaware. She designed the cover for *Rooster in the Hen House.*

Gemelle John has performed and facilitated poetry performances throughout Delmarva since 2014. In 2018, she was named a Delaware Division of the Arts Fellow in Literature (emerging poet category. She is a Vona alumnus and has received fellowships from Juniper and the Delaware Seashore Poetry & Prose Writers' Retreat sponsored by the Delaware Division of the Arts. Her work has been published or is upcoming in *Cleaver Magazine*, *Public Pool*, *The News Journal* (delawareonline.com), and *Beltway Quarterly*.

Larry Kelts, a retired research scientist, has published poetry in a number of journals including, *The Broadkill Review*, *miller's pond*, *Hazmat Review*, *Straitjackets*, *Chantarelle's Notebook*, and *Slipstream*. He is also the author of *Tatters*, a chapbook published by Foothills Publishing. For over five years, he has been working on a long poem tentatively titled "Lost in the Lewis & Clark Water Park." Sections in this anthology are part of that long poem. He lives in Newark, Delaware, with his wife, Diane.

TJ Lewes (Tanya Schuler-Koltuk) is currently writing two novels and has published several short stories. Her most recent publications include; *El Día de Los Angelitos Inocentes*, *The Snow Monkey*, *Pysanky Spring*, and *The Windchime*. In 2018, she won a Judge's Award for *Chicken and French Fries* and was one of 11 prose writers chosen for the Delaware Seashore Poetry & Prose Writers' Retreat sponsored by the Delaware Division of the Arts. She is certified in skydiving and scuba, and has lived in Spain, traveled throughout Central and South America, and has taught and traveled throughout China. She is now embracing her biggest adventure: raising two children in Sussex County, Delaware.

Maria Masington is a poet, author, and spoken word artist from Wilmington, Delaware. Her poetry has appeared in over a dozen publications including, *The Fox Chase Review*, *Adanna*, *The News Journal*, and *Earth's Daughters*. She has had five short stories published in anthologies through Smart Rhino Publications and Cat & Mouse Press. She is a member of Written Remains Writers Guild, The Mad Poet Society, and is "Your Friendly Emcee" and featured poet on the local art scene. She has been a guest on WVUD ArtSounds and is a three-time fellow at the Delaware Seashore Poetry & Prose Writers' Retreat.

Jennifer Morrell works as a public interest attorney. Prior to law school, she worked as a business writer and newspaper copy editor. Jen has completed NaNoWriMo twice, and in 2016 she attended her first Delaware Seashore Poetry & Prose Writers' Retreat sponsored by the Delaware Division of the Arts, a valuable experience that introduced her to Delaware's welcoming writing community. Last summer, she directed (along with her daughter) a play she wrote as part of the Wilmington Drama League's Jeff Walker One Act Festival.

Alice Morris's poetry has appeared in the *Paterson Literary Review*, *Gargoyle*, *Backbone Mountain Review*, *Rat's Ass Review*, *The Broadkill Review*, and in numerous anthologies. She was named a Pushcart Prize finalist (2019) and nominated for The Best of the Net Award (2019). Also an artist, her work has been published in *The New York Art Review* and *West Virginia Studies Our Heritage*. In 2018, she won the Florence C. Coltman Award for Creative Writing, and was short-listed (2018) for *Postcard, Poems, and Prose's* short-fiction contest.   In the Delaware Press Association's Communication Contest (2018), she received second place for poetry and third place for prose. She has work forthcoming in *The Broadkill Review*, *Paterson Literary Review*, and *Gargoyle*.

John Newlin has completed post-graduate studies at the Bread Loaf School of English, the University of Massachusetts, and earned his MFA in fiction writing at Converse College (SC). His work has appeared in *South 85*, *Night Owl*, *Short Story America*, *Work in Progress*, and *Independent School Magazine*. In addition to co-editing this anthology, he has served as an editor of *South 85*. His book reviews appear in the *New York Journal of Books*.

Leslie Pietrzyk is the author of the novel *Silver Girl*, which Publishers' Weekly called "profound, mesmerizing, and disturbing," and the novels *Pears on a Willow Tree* and *A Year and a Day*. Her collection of unconventionally linked short stories, *This Angel on My Chest*, won the 2015 Drue Heinz Literature Prize and was published by the University of Pittsburgh Press. Short fiction/essays have appeared in *Ploughshares*, *Washington Post Magazine*, Salon, *Southern Review*, *Gettysburg Review*, *Hudson Review*, *The Sun*, *Shenandoah*, *Arts & Letters*, *River Styx*, *Iowa Review*, *The Collagist*, and *Cincinnati Review*. She teaches fiction in the Converse College low-residency MFA program in South Carolina, and she lives in Alexandria, Virginia.

Russell Reece's poems, stories and essays have appeared in a variety of journals and anthologies including, *Blueline*, *The 3288 Review*, *Memoir Journal*, *Crimespree Magazine*, *Edify Fiction*, *Under the Gum Tree*, *The Broadkill Review*, and others. Russ has received fellowships in literature from The Delaware Division of the Arts and the Virginia Center for the Creative Arts. He recently won the Pat Herold Nielsen Poetry Prize in Chester River Art's 2019 Art of Stewardship contest. His stories and poetry have received Best of the Net nominations, awards from the Delaware Press Association and the Faulkner-Wisdom competition. Russ lives in rural Sussex County near Bethel, Delaware, on the beautiful Broad Creek.

Leslie J. Sysko is the author of *Battledore* (Finishing Line Press, 2017), a poetry chapbook. Her work has been published in *Best New Poets 2013*, *Ploughshares*, *Rattle*, *Day One*, *5am*, and other print and online journals. A recipient of both Emerging Artist and Opportunity grants from Delaware's Division of the Arts, she received an MFA in poetry at New England College in 2006. She has studied at conferences, workshops, and master classes ranging from Breadloaf and Colrain to the University of Nebraska and Key West. In addition to writing poetry, she writes fiction and non-fiction. In 2016, she won an honorable mention in Zoetrope's All-Story contest judged by Anthony Marra. She is English department chair at Tower Hill School in Wilmington, Delaware.

Susan L Towers writes fiction and nonfiction. She contributes to *Delaware Beach Life* magazine and writes a monthly blog for Beebe Healthcare's Women's Health website. In 2010, she received the Florence Coltman Award for Creative Writing for her essay, *Over the Rainbow*, which appeared in *No Place Like Here: An Anthology of Southern Delaware Poetry and Prose*. More recently, her first fiction story, *Harry's Pickup*, was published in *Scenes, A Collaboration of Coastal Writers and Artists*. She previously worked as a reporter and editor, winning several awards: including, First Place environmental category, newspapers 75,000 to 200,000 circulation, awarded by the California Newspaper Publishers Association, and the George F. Gruner Award for meritorious public service in journalism, awarded by the McClatchy Newspaper organization.

Billie Travalini's work has been published in *The Moth, Another Chicago Magazine, Things Left and Found by the Side of the Road, Lakeview International Journal of Literature and Arts*, and *The Journal of Caribbean Literatures*, among others. Her memoir, *Blood Sisters*, was a finalist for the Bakeless Publication Prize and won the Lewes Clark Discovery Prize. Her edited work incudes *On the Mason Dixon Line: an Anthology of Contemporary Delaware Writers* (with Fleda Brown), *No Place Like Here: An Anthology of Southern Delaware Poetry and Prose*, and *Teaching Troubled Youth: A Practical Pedagogical Guide*. She is a recipient of the Governor's Award for the Arts, Education and the Delaware Division of the Arts, Masters Award in Literature. A longtime advocate for at-risk kids and the mentally ill, she is the co-founder and coordinator of the Lewes Creative Writers Conference, teaches creative writing at Wilmington University and is busy at work on *Rush Limbaugh and the French Apple Pie and Other Stories*, and *Rules to Survive Childhood*, a sequel to *Blood Sisters*.

Jean Youkers work has been published in *Delaware Beach Life* magazine, *Cicada's Cry micro-zine, Dreamstreets*, and *The Broadkill Review*. She has also been published in thee anthologies, *Beach Days, Beach Love*, and *Beach Fun*. She is a member of the Wright Touch Writing Group and loves to write fiction, humorous nonfiction, and poetry. In keeping with her retirement mission of promoting humor and optimism, she leads humor-writing workshops at Osher and elsewhere.